HERE & NOW

Contemporary Tapestry from: Australia,
Canada, Finland, Japan, Latvia, Norway,
United Kingdom, United States

Edited by Lesley Millar

HERE & NOW

Contempory Tapestry from: Australia, Canada, Finland, Japan, Latvia, Norway, United Kingdom, United States

Published by	National Centre for Craft and Design.
Editor	Lesley Millar
Editorial Assistant	Christine Day
Line Editor	June Hill
Designer	Gerry Diebel
Design and Production	www.directdesign.co.uk
Print	www.fox-ms.co.uk
Japanese Translations	Mary Murator: mhm-translation@hotmail.com

Here And Now Team

Lesley Millar (Curator), Bryony Windsor (Head of Exhibitions NCCD), Keiko Kawashima (Co-ordinator Japan)

ISBN 978-1-5262-0454-7

CONTENTS

EXHIBITION DATES

National Centre for Craft and Design, Sleaford
1st October 2016 - 15th January 2017

mac Birmingham
1st April 2017 - 4th June 2017

The Holburne Museum, Bath
24th June 2017 - 1st October 2017

ARTISTS

ACKNOWLEDGEMENTS

The impetus for this exhibition began several years ago - walking through the night time streets of Kyoto with Fiona Rutherford after the opening of the wonderful tapestry exhibitions organised by Keiko Kawashima, Yasuko Fujino and Valerie Kirk. It had been a revelation to discover the group of young Japanese tapestry artists and Fiona and I discussed how we might bring the work to the UK. So a huge thank you to the National Centre of Craft and Design, for the opportunity to celebrate woven tapestry in the form of this exhibition. In particular Head of Exhibitions Bryony Windsor for her unstinting support throughout. Thanks also to Liz Cooper for starting the collaboration on its way. Thank you to the University for the Creative Arts for the continuing support for my research and in particular for the research and development for this exhibition. Thank you to all our funders and sponsors - the exhibition could not have happened without you. Thank you, as ever, to Gerry Diebel and his team at Direct Design for the advice and input which has resulted in yet another beautiful catalogue, and special thanks to Christine Day for her hard work and support in pulling the catalogue together. Thank you Keiko Kawashima for your advice and hard work. And most especially thank you to all the artists for their enthusiasm and commitment to woven tapestry - long may it continue.

Lesley Millar

Celebrating the *Here & Now*

The National Centre for Craft & Design (NCCD) is proud to host 'Here & Now' - an exhibition of international contemporary tapestry, curated in partnership with Professor Lesley Millar, unrivalled in her reputation for contemporary textile research. NCCD has a longstanding relationship with Lesley hosting '21:21 - the textile vision of Reiko Sudo and NUNO' in 2006 and the UK premier of her exhibition 'Cultex: Textile as cross cultural language', in 2010.

'Here & Now' is an ambitious survey of contemporary tapestry today – celebrating its importance and relevance and marking a moment in time for the medium.

As a venue NCCD is committed to championing national and international craft and design. Renowned for its commitment to textiles this will be NCCD's first exploration of tapestry and it is a privilege to dedicate the Main Gallery to international stars who are creating inspiring, provocative, exquisite and daring tapestries of our time.

Each of the exhibition pieces has been carefully selected for its individual merit and ability to mark a point in time in the artist's career, in textiles and in the modern world. The show presents a diverse mix of UK artists alongside talent from seven other countries, emphasising that the art of tapestry weaving is contemporary and relevant nationally and internationally.

Opportunities to work with new funding partners - the Daiwa Anglo-Japanese Foundation; the Great Britain Sasakawa Foundation and the University for the Creative Arts, enables curators and artists to engage in international exchange and debate through this thought provoking exhibition.

At a time of global uncertainty, the focus on the here and now and its legacy is more pertinent than ever. 'Here & Now' is a point in time for further research, practice and the promotion of cross cultural networking and greater experiential opportunities for contemporary tapestry.

BRYONY WINDSOR
Head of Exhibitions
The National Centre for Craft & Design

Weaving tapestry is a magical act of melding yarns to create a mural full of power and subtlety. Joanne Saroka[1]

TAPESTRY - HERE & NOW

As our lives become more instant and the news becomes more demanding and ever present, the time for reflection is hard to find. This exhibition offers the view that there is a potent space for woven tapestries[2] to occupy, to hold and to tell the story of our times.

Woven tapestry is formed from the most basic construction: hand manipulated warp and weft. To weave a tapestry is an intensely intimate act; the weaver must concentrate on tiny areas at a time, building shape upon shape of imagery, colour and narrative, until the final, and usually large scale, work is completed. Examples range from the 4th or 5th century Coptic tapestries with their bold imagery, to the highly complex early 16th century European tapestries telling the story of 'The Lady and The Unicorn', and reaching forward to the energetic and vibrantly coloured works of studio artists in the late 20th century.

Here in the UK we have a proud history for the commissioning and appreciation of tapestries since the Middle Ages. After the Second World War there was a re-positioning of tapestry as an expressive medium in its own right, rather than an interpretation of great artists paintings, which gathered momentum in the late 1960's into the 1970's. The movement became a real concentration of energy through to the mid 1990's. This was also true in the Nordic countries, in continental Europe, in the USA, in the Soviet Union, and in Australia and New Zealand.

Of course there were different social and economic circumstances in all these countries which directly affected this interest, including a percent for art in new buildings. Here in England in the 1970's many of the newly qualified textile makers were responding to the opportunities available through the discovery by architects of the wonderful conversation between soft textiles and hard edged buildings. The result was an explosion of contemporary tapestries that excited and seduced architects, artists and the public.

And then, as things do, the focus shifted; tapestries take so long to make, they aren't economic. The flagship international event, the Lausanne Tapestry Biennale, became more and more engaged with the new technologies that were offering previously unimagined possibilities. It wasn't an immediate change, more of a slow burn; people needed to earn a living, wanted to experiment, to connect more fully with three dimensionality, with space, with technology. Finally most of the courses teaching woven tapestry closed down. After a while one looked around and found an absence. As Jessica Hemmings observed in 2013: 'It is fair to concede that tapestry is a road far less travelled these days.'[3]

The seeming disappearance of woven tapestry from the public stage coincided with a time when the actual and metaphorical relationship between cloth and narrative was being explored in depth by artists, curators and writers. Yet, paradoxically, what was overlooked during these years was that aspect of textile art which had been developed with specific narrative intention: woven tapestry. However, this did not, and does not, represent an absence of new work; textile artists have continued to weave tapestries. In the UK, throughout Europe, Scandinavia, Australia, the USA, Canada and many of the Latin American countries the art of tapestry weaving flourishes, with Japan also now home to an energetic new interest in the art, particularly amongst young artists.

'Here and Now' represents an opportunity to think about that energy and how we can re-connect and regenerate the excitement in the medium. The first questions must be: is tapestry relevant? would there be interest? and I would answer a resounding yes. There is a societal hunger for textural experience - on a superficial level witness the constant caress of the screen - coupled with a desire for the personalised and unique expression, which finds correspondence with time-based/handmade activity. What is necessary is to find ways in which tapestry becomes the subversive membrane between the virtual and the textural, the instant and the long term, the hasty and the considered.

It is that notion of 'subversive' that links the future to the past. At the same time that Roszika Parker's 'Subversive Stitch', published in 1984, changed the context in which embroidery was researched, taught and practiced, tapestry weavers began to overtly reflect issues of concern: feminism, the environment, gender politics, cultural identity. This was achieved through connection to a different narrative history of their medium. For example Hannah Ryggen who was born in 1894 and ran a small farm on a remote Norwegian fjord. Her domestic life prefigured the aspirations for sustainability which are embraced today. Her husband built her loom and she used her own natural dyes in a conscious attempt to live in harmony with nature. She was also politically engaged - a left wing pacifist at a time of great upheaval: the 1930's and 40's. She used her tapestries to voice dissent against the rise of Fascism. For instance her tapestries which honoured Norwegian resistance to the occupation or depicting the beheading of a young mother - a Communist sympathiser.

Not all her work was so dark in subject matter but even her romantic piece about love and progress 'We are living on a star' became, unwittingly, a comment on the worst that man can do to man. It was commissioned for the Parliament Building in Oslo and it was damaged when Anders Breivik Behring's mini-van filled with 950 kgs of explosives blew up the Parliament Building on 22 July 2011 killing 8 people, injuring thirty more. Breivik then went on to massacre the 69 school children and teachers at the youth summer camp on the island of Utöya. As was said at the time: the art of Ryggen represents exactly what Breivik wanted to destroy. In this case he failed. 'We are living on a star' will soon be shown again, with the damage visible, and as such the tapestry fulfils and extends its role as carrier of narrative.

Hannah Ryggen's work demonstrates that tapestry as an expression of those socio-political aspects of life which are of importance/concern, has its own history. Within this exhibition 'Here and Now: contemporary woven tapestry' there are those who represent these different areas of engagement - with urban realities, or rural longings. Alongside the British tapestry weavers the exhibition features those from Australia, Canada, Norway, Finland, Japan, Latvia and the USA. In this way the exhibition demonstrates the international interest in contemporary tapestry and the ways in which the narrative heritage of the medium is used to engage with political, aesthetic and personal issues of current discourse. The works are witty, painful and beautiful, reflecting the power and harmony of nature,

social concerns and fears for the future of the world. They also, as Sharon Marcus has commented about exhibiting Canadian artist Barbara Heller: 'raise more questions than they answer, but they are provocative and disarming in their beauty, and thus have great potential for subversive communication.' [4]

And so we return to the subversive. The artists in this exhibition represent, but do not define, an international cohort who are committed to tapestry weaving and who refuse to sit still, who are constantly pushing boundaries and perceptions, producing beautiful and challenging work. There are many such artists, too many for one exhibition, thank goodness. Older artists who crafted their skills during the spotlight years, and young ones who, against the odds, are working in the medium. They are all excited, dedicated and creating tapestries that are as reflective of the times we live in now, as the tapestries produced across the centuries were of their times.

PROFESSOR LESLEY MILLAR
July 2016

Curator HERE & NOW
Director, International Textile Research Centre
University for the Creative Arts

REFERENCES

1. Joanne Saroka (2011) Tapestry Weaving: Design and Technique. Marlborough UK. The Crowood Press Ltd. P3

2. To write of 'woven tapestry' is something of a tautology as the definition of a tapestry is a woven cloth where the weft does not run continuously from selvedge to selvedge. Tapestry is described here in this way to differentiate from embroidered needlepoint which is sometimes referred to as 'tapestry work'

3. http://jessicahemmings.com/index.php/tag/tapestry/#_edn1. Visited 2.8.15

4. Sharon Marcus, lecture for American Tapestry Alliance conference as quoted on http://barbaraheller.ca/news-reviews/ Visited 8.6.16

SARA BRENNAN **UK**

A band of trees, a band of rain, a line of thought.

My work is always an unspoken response to landscape; a considered reflection and an expression of place. It is deeply rooted in the Scottish landscape; its prevailing presence, environments and forms. It is understated and uses a simple palette.

The tapestries (Gobelin technique) are taken from drawings, exploring the drawn mark and translating this drawn mark into a woven surface. This surface is unique to tapestry and becomes a woven mark in its own right. It is not a 'copy' of a drawn mark in yarn, the intention is to use the yarn as a painter would use paint or a printmaker use inks. The complexities of this surface means these tapestries take a very long time to weave.

I often obsess about the inherent capabilities and qualities of a specific yarn. By weaving, for example, an old French wool next to a different type and colour of yarn, it will alter the surface and change both their qualities. Sample after sample is woven until it all falls into place and makes sense in a particular piece of work. This can be very frustrating as the yarn is often old and unreplaceable, the amount that I have dictating the size and scale of the final piece. Some of these yarns have been given and some were inherited from my father's studio in Edinburgh. They all have a previous history and it is the inherent quality and colour of these older tapestry yarns that are exciting.

Each new body of work brings a slight shift within its content. Currently I have been working with groups of trees in my drawings. These 'forests' help articulate another understanding of the layers of dialogue within a northern landscape.

RECENT EXHIBITIONS INCLUDE

2016   Browngrotta Arts, Connecticut, USA: Artboom
2016   The Scottish Gallery, Edinburgh Distilled Tone-Showcase Sara Brennan
2015   VAS, RSA, Edinburgh: Cordis Award
2015   European Tapestry Forum, touring Finland, Germany, Austria and Denmark: Artapestry
2015   Watermill Gallery, Aberfeldy: Thinking and Making - Four Artist Weavers

RECENT AWARDS INCLUDE

2016   Creative Scotland: Artistic Development Award
2015   Shortlisted for Cordis Trust, VAS
2008   Jerwood Contemporary Makers Award
2005   Scottish Arts Council: Artistic Development Award

ALBA | CHRUTHACHAIL

TITLE: Deep Forest with Old Blue/Grey band (detail)
SIZE: 72 x 95 cm
MATERIALS: linen, wool, cotton

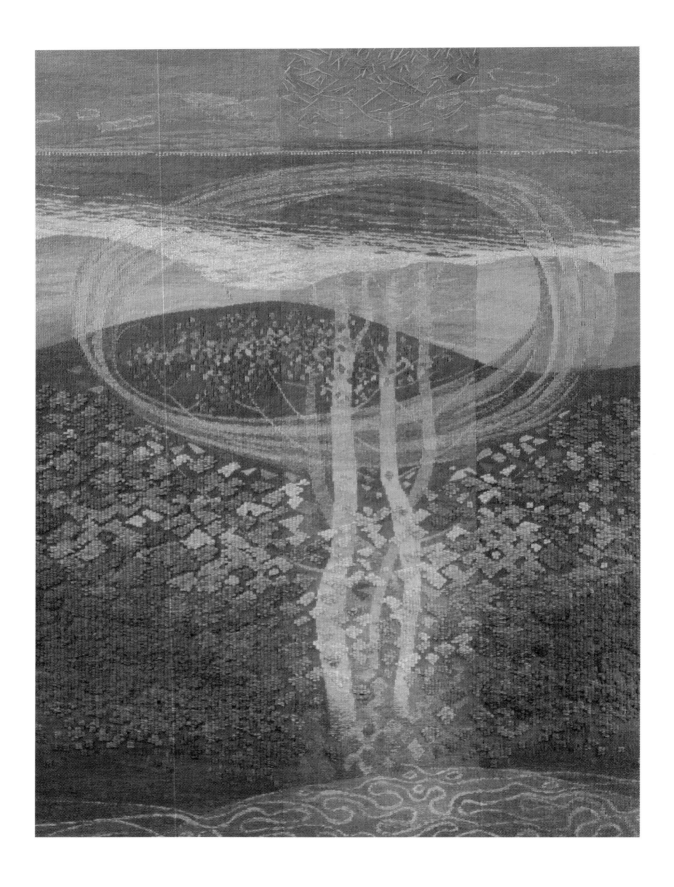

TITLE: Halaig 2 (detail)
SIZE: 196 cm x 188 cm
MATERIALS: wool, silk, lurex

JOAN BAXTER **UK**

Halaig 2

Inspired by the landscapes and cultural heritage of the far north of Scotland where I live, I use the ancient technique of tapestry weaving to explore my world.

After studying tapestry at Edinburgh College of Art and Warsaw Academy of Fine Arts during the 1970's, I spent eight years working as a weaver and trainer in commercial tapestry studios in the UK and Australia, notably working on the Henry Moore tapestries at West Dean Tapestry Studio.

I have been an independent tapestry artist since 1987, working to commission and exhibiting widely. I have had solo exhibitions in the UK and Denmark and participated in many group exhibitions around the world. Among my many commissioned works are pieces for churches, corporate and private clients.

Committed to raising critical awareness of tapestry and passing on skills, I lecture and teach regularly in Europe and North America. I also mentor individuals, curate exhibiting projects and am active in various artist-led groups.

My work is designed to be subtle, thoughtful and subliminal and I intend it to speak powerfully to people on an emotional level.

The landscapes of the far north have a particular minimal beauty and are strongly atmospheric. Tapestry designs rarely start with a beautiful view. The origin is usually more nebulous, less visual, often a mood evoked by a place, a text or a piece of music. My interests in archaeology, ecology and history combined with walks to explore these aspects in my local landscapes and other places all feed into what I make.

At the outset I have no clear picture of how a finished tapestry will look as the piece develops and changes during the weaving. I find the measured pace and technical constraints of weaving curiously liberating and only when I am weaving do the really good ideas come to me, so my work could never exist in any other medium.

I am increasingly interested in exploring less traditional approaches to my medium, experimenting with technique and materials and collaborating with others. I want to make work that pushes boundaries whilst retaining the beauty and expressive power of the traditional tapestry form.

This tapestry is my second piece inspired by the poem, 'Halaig' by Sorley MacLean. In it the poet describes how the empty landscape of his ancestral home is haunted by memories of the people who once lived there. For me, the poem captures exactly the atmosphere of the ruined villages and lost fields I encounter whilst walking in my own landscape.

RECENT EXHIBITIONS INCLUDE

2016   Interconnections, tapestries from Scotland and Ireland, Roscommon, April/May, co-curator (Group)

2015   Contemporary International Tapestry, Hunterdon Art Museum, New Jersey, USA, curated by Carol Russell (Group)

2014   The Weaver, Luddes Hus Gallery, Laesoe Island, Denmark (Solo)

2012/13 Timelines, collaboratively designed and woven tapestry with Irish tapestry weavers

2012/ONGOING Homework Project, annual international weaving, learning, networking and exhibiting project for student groups and professional tapestry weavers, touring to Denmark, Orkney, Yorkshire, Ireland, Faroes and New England

www.joanbaxter.com

JILLY EDWARDS **UK**

Within the Walls

This is about the surface, its depth, its construction, and the quiet. Crisp whites, sensuous dark colours, the rich warm yellows.

The space between the sections holds particular importance, the line on the horizon, where the solidity of the earth meets the changing skies. What is it between? A reflection to look into and what you see back. I was inspired by a stay on the Lizard Peninsula, Cornwall, famed for its wild and remote environs, staying in an ancient farmstead surrounded by dry stonewalls, covered in lichens. The lichens were a stunning splash of yellow amongst the dark stones walls and the dark rolling fields of corn and wild grasses with racing white clouds.

RECENT EXHIBITIONS INCLUDE

2015   CAA, London, New Makers
2015   Walford Mill Craft Centre, Wimborne Minster, Dorset
2014   Touchstones Rochdale Gallery, Rochdale, Lancashire
2014   Project Space, COLLECT, Saatchi Gallery, London
2014   Harley Gallery, Welbeck, Nottinghamshire, (Solo) Wanderlust

RECENT AWARDS INCLUDE

2016/17 Arts Council England
2016   Madeleine Mabey Trust
2015   Heritage Craft Association. Highly Commended. Maker of the Year
2014   Arts Council England, COLLECT

www.jillyedwards.co.uk

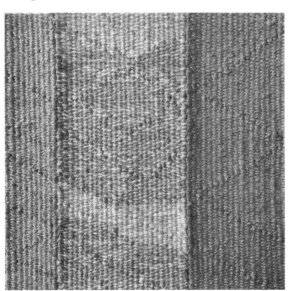

TITLE: Within the Walls, Kestle Barton (left & detail above)
SIZE: 160 x 160 cm
MATERIALS: cotton warp, wool, cotton, linen weft

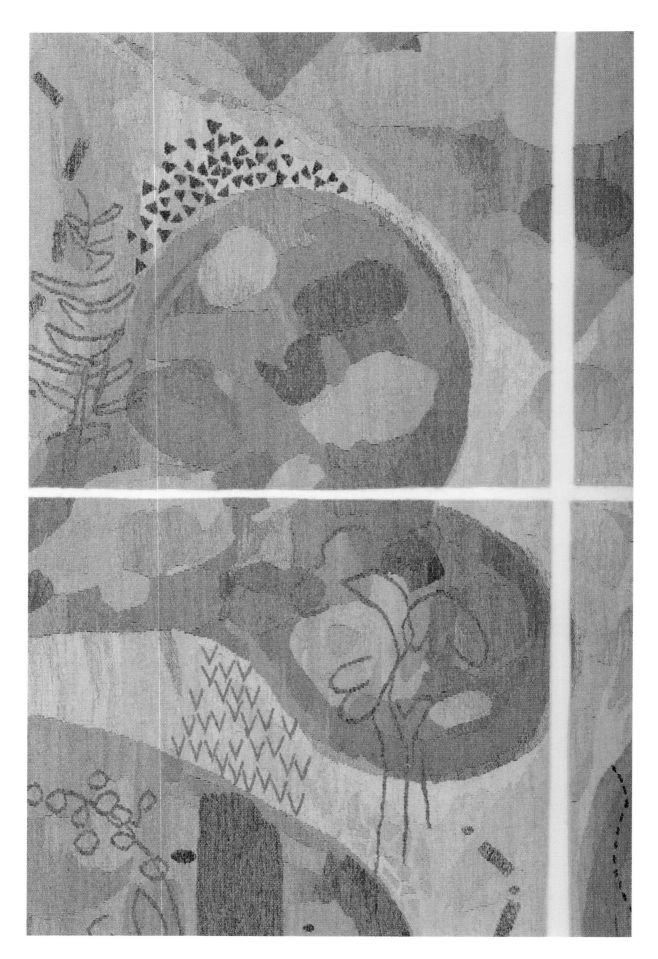

YASUKO FUJINO **JAPAN**

In the garden

When I am in this place, I lose all sense of time; my sense of where I am and what I am doing becomes blurred. I no longer have a sense of whether things around me are large or small, near or far, or even if they are there at all. For me, the 'garden' is a boundary between the everyday and the extraordinary. In this piece, I explore the disjunction and overlap between memory and my present continuous self, as if spinning a story through weaving. A woven piece is created by the intersections of the warp and weft. In my weaving, I feel that the intersection of memory and reality in the same plane are expressing a place where there is an honest version of myself.

I always explore new possibilities of expression through weaving. As I work, there are moments where ideas - images and materials - come to me suddenly and wonder "how would it be if I did this?" These ideas are not given to me from another world, but based on my own experience and knowledge and small things around me. Even tiny things by my feet can sow the small seeds in my mind. During the long process of weaving I can express so many different worlds.

Tapestry has the qualities of both flatness and three dimensions, and this produces a unique space. Even in the days when the role of tapestry was to tell a story, it possessed the ability to lead the viewer to a special artistic space. Even now, the best tapestries not only demonstrate the artistic abilities of the creator, but have the capacity to spin a story in the space created by the weaving in collaboration with the viewer.

RECENT EXHIBITIONS INCLUDE

2015   Kawaii: crafting the Japanese culture of cute
        (James Hockey and Foyer Galleries UCA/UK)
2013   Cloth & Memory {2} Salts Mill, Saltaire,
        Yorkshire UK
2013   Kauno Biennial - Tapestry Nova
        (Kaunas:Lithuania)
2012   International Tapestry Exhibition
        (Kyoto Art Center)
2008   Tapestry 2008 (The Australian National
        University School of Art Gallery)

TITLE: In the garden (detail)
SIZE: 250 x 410 cm
MATERIALS: silk, metal thread, mohair

TITLE: Ozymandias

SIZE: 158 x 168 cm

MATERIALS: Linen warp, hand-dyed commercial and hand-spun wool, cotton, and miscellaneous fibres, bones

BARBARA HELLER **CANADA**

Ozymandias

People bury land mines and then people bury the victims of land mines. What are we doing to our world and what are we doing to each other?

Land mines and the devastation they cause are a potent symbol of how the innocent suffer from the effects of war –most victims of land mines are children and the elderly who unwittingly stray into an unmarked mine field. Man thinks he is in control of his world but unexpected natural disasters and predictable (and preventable) man-made disasters are equally deadly. This quote from a poem by Shelley epitomizes such hubris.

> ...'My name is Ozymandias, King of Kings:
> Look upon my works, ye Mighty, and despair!
> Nothing beside remains. Round the decay
> Of that colossal wreck, boundless and bare
> The lone and level sands stretch far away.'

Along the bottom of the tapestry, in blue-green boxes are the land mines, hidden and deadly. I have woven them as drawings and used metallic threads to emphasize their man-made nature.

Above lies a rag doll with gingham and hearts referring to the innocence of childhood. Lost limbs are the primary result of a land mine. The doll lies in a vast desert, a wasteland with distant buildings on the horizon lit up by tracer fire in a night sky. The tracer bullets can be seen as fireworks and I used shiny yarns to make them more festive, a contrast to their true purpose.

For me the bird is the angel of death, menacing and lethal, but it could also be seen as an avenging angel crying out in anguish over what man has wrought, or a mother bird crying out a warning. The arrangement of the bird's feathers and their vibrant colours are at odds – is the bird alive or dead? Is this apocalyptic future inevitable?

RECENT EXHIBITIONS INCLUDE

2016   15th International Triennial of Tapestry, Lódz, Poland

2016   American Tapestry Biennial 11, South Bend Museum of Art, Indiana and touring to Topeka, Kansas and San Jose, California

2015   Contemporary International Tapestry, Hunterdon Art Museum, Clinton New Jersey

2014   Falling from Grace, Maple Ridge Art Gallery, Maple Ridge BC (Solo)

2010   From Lausanne to Beijing: 6th Biennial Textile Exhibition, Zhengzhou, China

RECENT AWARDS INCLUDE

2016   Teitelbaum Award –First Prize, American Tapestry Biennial 11

2009   Hilde Gerson Award for excellence, innovation and leadership in the BC craft community

1994   Recipient of a N'Shei Chabad Award for Women in the Arts for 'enriching the community'

www.barbaraheller.ca

TONJE HØYDAHL SØRLI **NORWAY**

We don`t know what the little bird sings!

My works are made with an interest in comics, and a fascination for popular culture. The sequential way of building a comic frame by frame is something I explore in tapestry and other works.

The warp and the back of my weavings are part of the finished work. This is the approach I take both to make the viewer curious about the technique, and point to the history of tapestry and needleworks. I try to focus on gender, trauma reactions, and relational balances of power in my works. Lately I`ve also worked with the idea of being an artist mother, and fear of indirectly harming one`s children through the choice of living a public role. This is theme in the piece 'Bloom! And Jolly Future!'

RECENT EXHIBITIONS INCLUDE

2016	Østlandsutstillingen, Akershus Kunstsenter, Lillestrøm
2015	Landart 2015, Ask, Gjerdrum
2015	The 5th Riga International Textile & Fibre Art Triennial, Riga
2014	Wearable Art Show, Knipsu, Bergen, Norway
2014	Solo Show, Galerie Chevalier, Paris, France

AWARDS INCLUDE

2002	Art Critic`s Prize, Trøndelagsutstillingen
2002	Tegneserieforbundet, Comic Book Story - Competition

www.tonjesorli.com.

TITLE: Bloom! And Jolly Future! (detail)
SIZE: 94 x 80 x 80 cm
MATERIALS: wool, cotton, linen

TITLE: We don`t know what the little bird sings!
SIZE: 300 x 80 x 60 cm
MATERIALS: wool, cotton, linen

TITLE: Tide
SIZE: 150 x 130 cm
MATERIALS: cotton warp, linen weft

FIONA HUTCHISON **UK**

Tide

The subject is The Sea, materials and medium are textile.

As an artist and teacher working predominantly, but not exclusively in Gobelin tapestry, content is paramount in the development of my work. I aim to create a dialogue between the subject, materials and the viewer. While traditional techniques and craftsmanship are important it is the idea, the vision and my hand that defines the work.

Growing up in the city, but by the waters edge, the sea is enormously important in my life. Over the last 30 years it has provided me with a starting point for my creative journey, whether from personal experience or research in all things maritime and marine. My aim is not to create a representation of the seas and oceans but something experienced, a deeply felt personal connection. It is as much a self portrait as it is a reflection on the sea.

The manipulation of materials and techniques increasingly plays an important role in the development of the work. Ideas take a long time to evolve, almost as long as it takes to weave them. They develop through a process of visual research: drawing, painting, sampling and experimenting with materials and techniques. I am inspired by the tactile qualities of woven surface, the delicacy of handmade paper from Nepal, or the translucency of architect's tracing paper. They all speak their own language, some will need no further development, others will cry out "weave me". This is the challenge.

'Tide' is part of a new collection of work that challenges me to explore the structure of tapestry and how it can be manipulated to represent my ideas: the ebb and flow of the tide, the oceans currents, whirlpools and maelstroms. These powerful bodies of water, that are constantly moving, constantly changing can be dangerous and unpredictable places, a possible metaphor for our current, political, cultural and ecological future. We must navigate with care.

RECENT EXHIBITIONS INCLUDE

2014	Uncharted Water (Solo Exhibition) Burghhall Gallery, Linlithgow
2013	International Paper Art, Sofia, Bulgaria Artapestry3, (European tour)
2011	Fountain Gallery, Piestany, Slovakia International Paper Art, Sofia, Bulgaria
2008	Across Boundaries, Soul, South Korea 7th Biennial of American Tapestry, USA
2007	5th Cheongju Biennial, South Korea 12th International Textiles Triennial, Poland

AWARDS INCLUDE

Arts Council England, Theo Moorman Trust, Hope Scott Trust, Hartlebury Foundation, Edinburgh Visual Arts & Craft Award, Sasakawa Foundation, Daiwa Foundation, Creative Scotland, Incorporation of Weavers

www.fionahutchison.co.uk

The Trades House of Glasgow

CUSTOMER SERVICE EXCELLENCE® CSE

AI ITO **JAPAN**

Baltic Travel Diary

The warp is the canvas, the weft is the paint. I choose the colours of the threads carefully as if I were mixing paints - gradually the colourless warp is buried beneath the weft. As time passes, so an image emerges from the accumulation of time. My work reflects my strong belief in the power that time holds.

For a number of years, I have used the motif of travel in my work. I ask myself why people are so drawn to travel. Because it takes you to an unfamiliar place away from your everyday life, perhaps? Or maybe because gradually you come to understand a strange place, a strange language, strange people and a strange culture. As I work, I try to capture the memories of that place that is not here.

'Baltic Travel Diary'

I travelled across three Baltic countries; from Tallinn in Estonia, through Riga in Latvia and Vilnius in Lithuania. Although each country shared the same red roofs and brick houses, each country was unique in its own way. My journey through these Baltic nations is told in my tapestry – the scenes going from left to right follow my route.

RECENT EXHIBITIONS INCLUDE

2016	15th International Triennial of Tapestry, Łódź 2016, Łódź, Poland (Selected)
2015	Yakudosuru Kansei Vol.1: Hello, Isetan Shinjuku 5F, Tokyo, Japan (Solo)
2015	Baltic travel diary, Gallerygallery Kyoto, Japan (Solo)
2015	Ori-rhythm III, Kyoto Art Center Kyoto, Japan (Group)
2014	Kyoto Arts and Crafts New Artist Exhibition, Japan (Selected)
2013	Tapestry Nova: Japan – Lithuania, Gallery Imeno Parkasi Kaunas, Lithuania (Group)
2013	9th Kaunas Biennial UNITEXT 2013, Kaunas, Lithuania (Selected)

AWARDS INCLUDE

2002	34th Mainichi DAS Gold Egg Prize, Textile Section, Section Prize

www.yaikora.com

TITLE: Baltic Travel Diary (above and details, left)
SIZE: 110 x 400 cm
MATERIALS: wool, cotton

AINO KAJANIEMI **FINLAND**

Golden Rain

My textiles are my way of thinking. I aspire to produce the objects of my wonderings into something concrete, so that I could understand them. I weave narratives where a person is in the middle of life's complexity and multi-layerism with her/his contrasts and controversies. I aspire for a little bit of order in my mind in the middle of a chaotic world.

I make pictures with small, concrete things using moments and atmospheres in a person's life, so that they form a metaphor of something greater. In my art I depict human growth and life's complex circumstances and emotions: longing, insecurity, fear, jealousy, joy, guilt, shame, success, the difficulty of communication and co-existence. Nowadays I think about the question of how a human being can find her/his place in the world, reverses, fears, needing support and dreams. My art isn't directly polemical or political but approaches the subjects more poetically and individually. I feel that even sad things are more easily approachable in textile because the material in itself holds optimistic and soft values.

I graduated in 1983 from the University of Arts and Design, Helsinki and I have worked as a free artist since 1990. I have taken part in numerous exhibitions in Finland and abroad, made several commission works and liturgical textiles for six churches.

RECENT EXHIBITIONS INCLUDE

2016 Stories of Migration: Contemporary Artists Interpret Diaspora, George Washington University, The Textile Museum, Washington, USA
2015 International tapestry exhibition, Hunterdon Art Museum, Clinton, New Jersey, USA
2014 Contextile 2014 – Contemporary Textile Art Biennial, Guimaraes, Portugal
2013 14th International Tapestry Triennial, Lodz, Poland
2012 International tapestry exhibition ORIZUME II, Kyoto Art Center, Japan
2005 -15 ARTAPESTRY, 1, 2, 3, 4 European Tapestry triennial, touring

RECENT AWARDS INCLUDE

2011-16 Personal five-year-grant for artistic work, Finland's National Council for Crafts and Design
2010 The textile artist of the year in Finland

www. elisanet.fi/aino.kajaniemi

TITLE: Golden Rain
SIZE: 164 x 164 cm
MATERIALS: linen, wool, cotton, hair, viscose, acrylic, gold thread

VALERIE KIRK **AUSTRALIA**

Floating Fossil

The work evolved from visits to the Age of Fishes Museum at Canowindra, NSW, Australia and it explores a fossil image translated through drawing into woven tapestry. The work embodies ideas about the distant past and our inability to fully visualise this as although we have remains, museum exhibits and artists' impressions, the reality of the past will always be beyond our grasp. The floating form alludes to a state of impermanence, transition and dislocation while the colour palette references an intangible space between water, earth and sky.

RECENT EXHIBITIONS INCLUDE

2015   Cordis Trust Prize for Tapestry, The Royal Scottish
        Academy, Edinburgh
2014   Botanic Art Exhibition, Australian National
        Botanic Gardens, Canberra
2014   Awaken, Craft ACT, Craft and Design Centre,
        Canberra
2009   Returning, Sturt Gallery, Mittagong
2006   Leaving and Returning, Warrnambool Art Gallery
2004   Journeys, Ararat Gallery

AWARDS INCLUDE

Current   Australia Council New Work Grant
2013   ACT Creative Arts Fellowship
2008   Energy Australia National Trust Heritage Award

TITLE: Floating Fossil (left and detail above)
SIZE: 100 x 100 cm
MATERIALS: wool, cotton

IEVA KRUMINA **LATVIA**

A Visitor from the Future

A visitor from the future is a 5000 year old
anthropomorphic artefact found in the Baltic territory;
it holds densely pressed information about the past, at
the same time retaining a formula that could be used by
the people of future.

TITLE: A Visitor from the Future
SIZE: 197 x 295 cm
MATERIALS: linen, wool, amber threads, silk, rayon,
nylon, polyester. Tapestry, applique, digital print, artist's
technique

RECENT EXHIBITIONS INCLUDE

2015   5th European Textile and Fiber Art Triennial,
Tradition & Innovation, Riga, Latvia
2014   International Lace Exhibition, Transparent
Structures, Riga, St. Peters' Church
2013   7th International Miniature Textile Exhibition,
Vilnius, Lithuania
2013   9th International Triennial of Textile Miniatures,
Gdynia, Poland
2011   Energy, International Miniature Textile
Exhibition, Como, Italy

AWARDS INCLUDE

2011   1st Diploma, Tapestry, International Art Festival,
Non-Forgotten Tradition, Moscow, Russia
2009   First Prize, The 6th International Biennial of
Textile Miniatures in Vilnius, Lithuania
2007   Special Prize, 5th Cheongju International Craft
Competition, Korea
2007   Prize of Distinction, 7th International Baltic
Mini Textile Triennial, Gdynia, Poland
2007   Prize of the Public, International Lace Biennial,
Heidelberg, Germany

www.ievakrumina.com

ROLANDS KRUTOVS **LATVIA**

Propera Ad Me (Come to me)

This is a fragile world of associations, full of reminiscences and future hopes. In the artwork 'Propera Ad Me', I am telling a story about Someone who is bravely following his path, although losing his balance at times. And there is Someone Else who is always standing nearby to guard with a glance, with loving past memories, emotions vanishing in dwindling tints of clouds and golden flickers of light.

Poetess' verses are a tribute to the one who years ago asked her to walk in the vast skies so as to finish with her queer habit of being alone. A long time has passed since then; it can't be measured in hours, minutes and seconds. It's only the story that has remained and a bizarre feeling of never-ending present and tiny golden flickers of each spent day.

> While pain dissolves in time like dust of sugar
> Solely feelings of the past happiness linger
> Gold colour on the Parisian blue
> Morning twilight and your turned away shoulders
> Are guarding my
> Overflowing in order
> Dream

TITLE: Propera Ad Me (Come to me)
SIZE: 126 x 130 cm
MATERIALS: cotton wool synthetics

RECENT EXHIBITIONS INCLUDE

2016   15th International Triennial of Tapestry, Łódź, Poland

2016   10th International Baltic Mini Textile Triennial, Gdynia, Poland

2016   24th International Contemporary Art Exhibition GEA,Como, Italy

2015   17th International Mini-Textile Exhibition, Memory of Textile, Bratislava, Slovakia

2014   8th International Fiber Art Biennale, From Lausanne to Beijing, Beijing, China

AWARDS INCLUDE

2011   Grand Prix Award, 21st International Contemporary Art Exhibition, Energhei, ARTE&ARTE

2010   Prize of Distinction, 8th International Baltic Mini-Textile Triennial

2009   Outside the Box/Craft Ideal Award, 6th Cheongju International Craft Competition

2005   Ansis Cīrulis' Award for the best figural textile composition of the year

2000   Grant awarded by the Latgale Culture and History Museum

AYAKO MATSUMURA **JAPAN**

I weave bodies. They represent the skin; the interface between a person's clothing and their body.

I chose skin because this is where, due to the skin's intimate relationship with both the inside and outside of the body, the effects of an individual's psychology, habits and age are most honestly displayed.

I am fascinated by the human custom of physical adornment and the constant search for beauty.

Thanks to advances in technology, the pursuit of human beauty can be taken increasingly far - even the shape of the human body itself can be transformed. Our relentless pursuit of beauty is pushing the boundaries of physical transformation, and there is no reason to think there will not be further developments in the future. By expressing the boundary between the body and clothing in my work, I am responding to the concept of the body and technology.

The reason I chose weaving as my medium of expression is, firstly, because of the fundamental essence of cloth as something to 'protect' and 'decorate' the body.

As humans, we take clothing for granted, and for this reason clothes and skin have evolved together. I wondered if, with the right materials and colours, I could use the unique qualities of weaving for creating images to represent the skin which forms the boundary between clothing and the body. By carefully manipulating the warp and weft, I create three dimensional images of the physical form of the body.

At present, the material I primarily work with is a yarn made from shredded animal skin. This material has a strength that you do not get with linen, cotton or silk. By replacing the human skin with the woven animal skin, I am drawing attention to the existence of human skin.

RECENT EXHIBITIONS INCLUDE

2016 Fabric, light and dirty, Artzone, Kyoto, Japan (Group)

2016 Kyoto City University of Arts Exhibition, Kyoto Municipal Museum of Art, Japan (Group)

2015 Contemporary Tapestry, Ori-rhythm III, Part 2 Kyoto Art Center, Japan (Group)

2014 Woman, Gallerygallery, Kyoto, Japan (Solo)

2014 Out of sight, Kunstarzt Kyoto, Japan (Solo)

AWARDS INCLUDE

2013 45th Mainichi / DAS Student Design Award Osaka, Japan, Golden Eggs Prize

2012 Kyoto City Exhibition, Kyoto, Japan, Director Encouraged Prize

2012 Seian University of Art and Design Graduate Exhibition, Kyoto, Japan, Excellence Prize

2012 2012 Kyoto City Exhibition, Japan, Selected

http://ayakomatsumura.tumblr.com

TITLE: Body Suit – Transformation (detail)
SIZE: 115 x 180 cm
MATERIALS: cotton, polythene, leather

TITLE: Golden Handshake
SIZE: 43 x 41cm
MATERIALS: wool, gold, cotton warp

CARON PENNEY **UK**

The streets are paved with gold

My artistic practice has evolved around a central theme of Manhattan since I first visited the city in 2001. I react to the urban landscape and the systems and patterns that repeat across the streets and avenues. Often these themes respond to the ebb and flow of the daily migration across the city. The subject matter draws comparisons between society's need to function and the individuals need for identity and their subtle co-existence. This careful balance is represented in the meticulous repetition of patterns and shapes in my tapestries. I reproduce familiar visual signs arranging them in sequences and rhythms.

> 'The Streets are Paved with Gold'
>
> 'Stop_Go_2008_2013'
>
> 'F**K OFF'
>
> 'Golden Handshake'

My latest work identifies with the extract, "the streets are paved with gold", from the 19th Century story of 'Dick Whittington', loosely based on the 14th century Lord Mayor of London, Richard Whittington. The ironic nature of these words became reality for me, when on the 15th September 2008 I unwittingly observed from the kerbside the employees of Lehman Brothers Holdings Inc. leaving their headquarters after the company had filed for bankruptcy. These events were to be seen by many as the beginning of the global financial crisis. I am now working on a series of tapestries using gold threads. The use of gold is a witty comment on events that have unravelled both globally and personally over the years that followed.

I explore duality such as lightness and heaviness, illusion and reality, obscenity and refined aesthetic. My work hovers between the abstract and the figurative, creating a window into a world which is both mysterious and familiar. In the tapestry 'Stop_Go_2008_2013' the text creates a sense of confusion which is intensional, and mirrors the emotions felt if made redundant from a company or community which a person once felt supported and nurtured by. Since the global financial crash in 2008

many people have endured the possibility of redundancy or been made redundant. This national and intentional joint experience is conveyed at its strongest in the tapestry 'F**K OFF'. Understandably this work can appear offensive but the lightness and refined aesthetic which envelope the work deliver the message with the same impact as a company who delivers a severance package to its employees.

RECENT EXHIBITIONS INCLUDE

2015   Manhattan Zimmer Stewart Gallery, Arundel, UK

2015   COLLECT 2015, Saatchi Gallery, London, UK
represented by the Wills Lane Gallery

2015   Craft Now, Shipley Art Gallery, Gateshead, UK

2015   The Wool Collection, Campaign for Wool
Southwark Cathedral, London, UK

2014   Summer Exhibition Royal Academy of Arts,
London, UK

www.weftfaced.com

ERIN M. RILEY **USA**

Self Portrait 1

I am a tapestry weaver that spends hours weaving on a floor loom using wool yarn that I hand dye, manipulate or deconstruct. I weave images of young women in states of undress or exposure, personal objects and various landscapes relating to destruction and death. I spend time researching addiction, sexual experimentation, popular internet culture, the effects of single parent households, socio-economic status etc.

I am drawn to images that represent sexuality as the private and intimate event that it sometimes can be but also finding the images that are the remnants of courtship, text message/IM/email flirtations turned into the litter of the internet or Facebook. I am using my own images that I have sent to lovers, and images of other women depicting the moments that I can relate to as a sexual being. I am also weaving the objects that I have formed attachments to, as well as objects that have had impacts in other people's lives, displays of arrests, deaths, addictions.

I am interested in the honesty of sexuality, but also how imagery, relationships, pornography and sex is changing as a result of the mass depiction of these intimate moments. I am interested in how my coming of age on the internet has affected the quality (or mere occurrence) of relationships. I am inspired by the beauty of a woman who takes a self portrait for her own pleasure and the pleasure of the ones she cares about, and all the people who get to glimpse into that moment and what they might say on message boards, comments and Twitter.

RECENT EXHIBITIONS INCLUDE

2016   You Can Call Me Baby, SPRING/BREAK Art Show, New York (Group)

2016   Landline: Works in Fiber from Coast to Coast, Praxis Fiber Workshop, Cleveland, Ohio (Group)

2015   Anew, Hashimoto Contemporary, San Francisco, California (Solo)

2015   Darkness Lies Ahead, Joshua Liner Gallery, New York (Solo)

2015   Data Flow: Digital Influence, Town Hall Gallery, Hawthorn, Victoria, Australia (Group)

2014   The Pain Comes in Waves, OGAARD Gallery, Oakland, California

2014   Crimson Landslide, Space 1026, Philadelphia

2013   Undo, University of Wisconsin Gallery, Oshkosh, Wisconsin (Solo)

RECENT AWARDS INCLUDE

2012   Ruth and Harold Chenven Foundation Grant, New York

2011   Vermont Studio Center Artist-in-Residence Full Fellowship, Johnson, Vermont

2011   Kittredge Foundation Grant Recipient, Cambridge, Massachusetts

2009   Best in Show, Radius 250, Artspace, Richmond, Virginia

TITLE: Self Portrait 1
SIZE: 182.88 x 121.92 cm
MATERIALS: wool, cotton

www.erinmriley.com

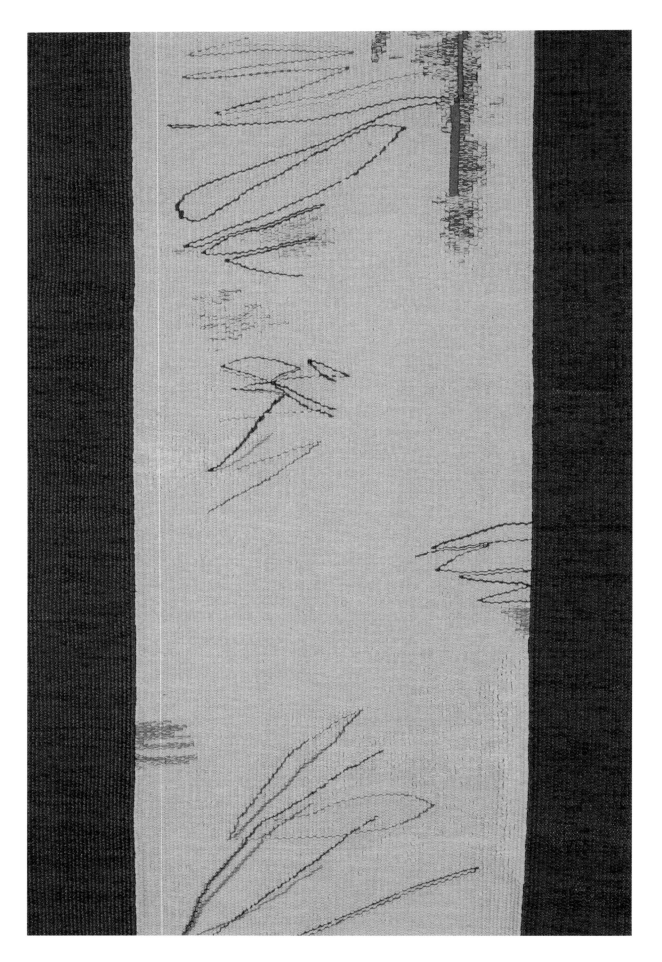

FIONA RUTHERFORD **UK**

All about everything

I love the emotional impact of colour, creating an immediate sense of energy through a vivid but limited colour palate. An intimacy of weaving and storytelling fascinates me, bringing together the past and present to create something new and still unfolding. My work is highly narrative and references people, music, words and events that are woven into the fabric of my tapestries. The imagery is a careful balance of patterns, symbols and mark making.

Life is a balancing act and this is reflected in my most recent work. Continuing to develop the theme of balance and space in marks and narrating major changes in my life that at once incite fear and thrill. Creative energy lost and found again.

RECENT EXHIBITIONS INCLUDE

2015   New Year Showcase, Contemporary Applied Arts, London
2012   Ori-Rhythm II, Kyoto Art Center, Kyoto, Japan
2011   COLLECT, Saatchi Gallery, London
2010   SOFA New York, (Represented by CAA Gallery, London)
2008   The Fine Art of Tapestry Weaving, ANU Canberra, Australia

RECENT AWARDS INCLUDE

2012   Arts Council Travel Award, Japan
2008   Arts Council/Prospect Travel Award, Australia
2005   Arts Council Research Award, Japan
2003   Arts Council Touring Exhibition Award
2002   Northern Arts Mentoring Scheme

www. rutherfordtextileart.com

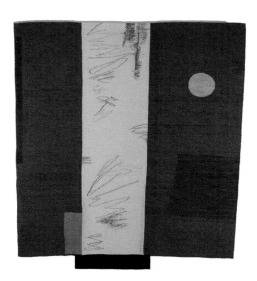

TITLE: All about everything (above and detail left)
SIZE: 130 x 110 cm
MATERIALS: cotton and linen yarn on cotton warp
IMAGES: Sally Jubb

KRISTIN SÆTERDAL **NORWAY**

New Territory

In the work 'New Territory' I'm continuing my exploration of the control room motif. It is a fairly large tapestry, 1.7 x 2.4 metres. The colours have darker tones and more nuances than in the former piece 'The Blue Control Room'. The ambience is of a world growing darker, but the untouched landscape is promising new beginnings and new territory. A new world to come.

TITLE: New Territory
SIZE: 1700 x 2400 cm
MATERIALS: wool, linen

RECENT EXHIBITIONS INCLUDE

2016   Gallleri BOA Oslo, Norway (Solo)
2016   Trondhjems Kunstforening, Trondheim, Norway (Solo)
2016   Nyfossum Blaafargeverket, Norway (Solo)
2015   Buskerud Artcenter, Norway (Solo)
2015   Extreme Fibers, Muskegon Art Museum, USA (Solo)

AWARDS INCLUDE

2015   Nominated for The Cordis Trust Prize for Tapestry, Scotland
2008   'Outstanding', 5th at Lausanne to Beijing, Textile and Fiber Biennal, China

www.kristinsaeterdal.com

SAORI SAKAI **JAPAN**

Let's Pretend

As I was making this piece, I wanted to create the feeling of modern everyday life through the innocence of children. When we use smartphones, tablets or other modern devices, we are quickly drawn from the real world into the virtual world of the internet, and I believe this is similar to the way children are drawn into a world of imagination or dreams. For me, this feels like a vague, strange world which defies logic. I have chosen motifs of surreal presences that inhabit this other world like monsters and fairies.

The materials I chose are artificial, such as nylon, and in fluorescent colours. I use them for the warp as they bring to mind the strong, bright, artificial lights of computer monitors and LCD screens that we encounter on a daily basis.

RECENT EXHIBITIONS INCLUDE

2016   Kite, Mite Nakanoshima2016, Ooebashi Station, Osaka, Japan (Group)

2015   Gotenyama Art Center for Lifelong Learning, Hirakata, Japan (Solo)

2015   Kite, Mite Nakanoshima2015, Nakanoshima Station, Osaka, Japan (Group)

2015   Ori-rhythmIII, Contemporary Tapestry, Kyoto Art Center, Kyoto, Japan (Group)

2014   Kyoten, Kyoto Municipal Museum of Art, Kyoto/2013,2012,2011,2010,2009,2008 (Group)

2014   Sakai City Exhibition, Sakai City Cultural Hall (Group)

2014   Kite, Mite Nakanoshima 2014, Naniwabashi Station, Osaka, Japan (Group)

AWARDS INCLUDE

2014   Sakai Mayor's Prize Sakai City Exhibition

2014   New Face Award, Sakai City Exhibition

2013   First Prize, All Kansai Exhibition

2012   Kasaku, All Kansai Exhibitions,

2011   Encouragement Prize, Kyoten

2009   First Prize, All Kansai Exhibition

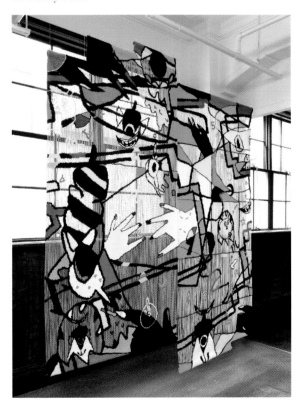

TITLE: Let's Pretend (above and detail, left)
SIZE: 2,500 x 2,200 cm
MATERIALS: nylon, wool, cotton

PHILIP SANDERSON **UK**

Windblown Tree

My current work is primarily concerned with the relationship between image and process. I usually work with photographs, the similarities in quality between the woven and pixelated image provides a useful starting point for translating the image into tapestry.

In 2014, with funding from the Theo Moorman Trust, I was able to develop my ideas for producing large scale tapestries with heavier, less conventional materials on a wider warp spacing to bring a greater dynamic and spontaneity to the weaving process and also to make more visible the structure of the tapestry.

Through experimental sample pieces I started to work with strips of fabric initially as a way of adding extra weight to the weft but soon recognised the potential for using printed fabric and the random effects that emerged when it is woven as a starting point for creating the palette of colours and tones for the tapestry. The fabric and other materials are combined with a series of coloured threads of 'found colour', i.e. not specifically dyed for the project, that help to link the different blends and materials together.

The resulting tapestries have much more of a physical presence and there are greater possibilities for interpreting the image which is informed partly by a basic cartoon, but equally by the limitations of the warp and weft settings.

TITLE: Windblown Tree (design above, detail below)
SIZE: 134 x 350 cm
MATERIALS: warp cotton, weft wool, cotton

RECENT EXHIBITIONS INCLUDE

2016   Converge, Cordis Trust Prize for Tapestry, Royal Scottish Academy, Edinburgh
2015   Healreef, West Dean College, Chichester
2014   Recording Britain Now: The John Ruskin Prize Millennium Gallery, Sheffield Museum
2014   The Open West, The Wilson, Cheltenham Art Gallery
2014   Music Makers, Bluecoat Display Centre, Liverpool
2013   The Power of Slow, online exhibition, American Tapestry Alliance
2013   Finding the Unicorn, Fleming Gallery, London
2011   Hatchet and Helve, Standpoint Gallery, London

AWARDS INCLUDE

2014   Theo Moorman Trust Award.
2010   Funded by the Newby Trust to research experimental tapestry weaving

www.philipsandersontapestry.com

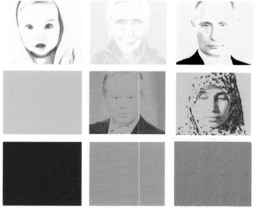

TITLE: 6704-13 (design left, detail above)
SIZE: 133 x 112 x 2 cm
MATERIALS: cotton, linen, wool

PAT TAYLOR **UK**

6704-13

In January 2015 Lesley Millar invited me along with 20 other tapestry weavers from all over the world, to exhibit in an international tapestry exhibition in the UK. My starting point was identity, our discontinuous and constructed histories, and how they are expressed in the landscape of the face. Juxtaposing, youth, middle age and old age, moving across both familiar and unfamiliar faces, I interspersed blank spaces of possibility, offering a canvas for the viewer to create a narrative, as we do in life. The hinterland of this work lies in recognising the veneer of civilisation, and the heart of darkness deep within what it is to be human.

- Discontinuous histories are forgotten, histories buried in the palimpsest of the `formative' values of the time.

- Looking back at my note books I came across this and it rang true:

We take home and language for granted; they become nature and their underlying assumptions recede into dogma and orthodoxy. The exile knows in a secular and contingent world, homes are always provisional. Borders and barriers, which enclose us within the safety of familiar territory, can become prisons, and are often defended beyond reason or necessity.
Reflections on Exile by Edward Said.

The exiled, which is most of us, can cross borders, both psychological and sociological and break through barriers of thought and experience.

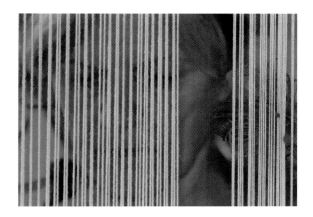

RECENT EXHIBITIONS INCLUDE

2015	Cordis, The Scottish Royal Academy, Edinburgh
2013	The Fleming Gallery, London
2009	COLLECT 2009, Saatchi Gallery, London
2008	The Fabric of Myth, Compton Verney, Warwickshire
2008	Interwoven, Grace Barrand Gallery, London
2008	COLLECT, V&A, London

COMMISSIONS

2004	GOSH project (collaborative project with the Slade School of Fine Art and Great Ormond St. Hospital)
2004	'Where Next', private client
2004	'Souvenir', private client
2002	'Bathroom Box', private client
1998	'Democracy 1&2', Portcullis House, Palace of Westminster

www.pat.taylor.com

MISAO WATANABE **JAPAN**

Red Scenery

Despite its beauty, the spider lily has a dark side; it is a poisonous plant which, according to folklore, will cause your house to burn down if you take it home. The sight of the blossoming spider lily always reminds me that humans, too, have two sides, and this is what stirred me to make my piece.

In Japan, we make a contrast between true feelings and public façade, preferring not to reveal our true thoughts, or express opinions that contradict those we are talking to. People who speak their mind are considered strange. Customarily, we gauge the reactions of those around us, take a breath and then say something vague and bland.

This is the life I lead. I think that foreigners sometimes find this custom difficult to understand.

All Japanese people exist in the space between public face and true thoughts: the conflict and agony of wanting to say something but being unable to speak the truth is an experience that is common to all Japanese people. Through weaving, I express the emotional rollercoaster, the stress, the depression, the anxiety, the irritation that arise from this; I have created an imagined scene entitled 'The Red Scenery'. Standing before this piece, viewers feel themselves being enveloped in the red colour of these strong emotions.

RECENT EXHIBITIONS INCLUDE

2016   Cordis Prize for Tapestry, Visual Arts Scotland Annual Exhibition, Edinburgh (Group)

2015   Riga International Textile and Fibre Art Triennial (Group)

2015   RINPA, 2015 Kyoto Art Kogei Biennale, Japan

2013   14th International Triennial of Tapestry, Lodz, Poland (Group)

2013   Tapestry Nova: Japan Lithuania, Kaunas (Group)

2012   Kyoto Art Kogei Biennale, Kyoto, Japan

2012   Ori - Rhythm II, Group Exhibition, Muromachi Art Court, Kyoto, Japan

AWARDS INCLUDE

2015   Riga International Textile and Fibre Art Triennial 3rd Prize

2006   Kyo-Ten Encouragement Award,

2006   From Lausanne To Beijing, Outstanding Award

2000   Kyo-Ten, Grand Prix Award

www.watanabe-misao.net

TITLE: Red Scenery
SIZE: 195 x 400 cm
MATERIALS: wool, cotton

AIMS

The National Centre for Craft & Design prides itself on being a world-class centre and resource dedicated to the celebration, support and promotion of national and international contemporary craft and design. We aim to stimulate greater understanding of contemporary craft and design and provide enriching arts and cultural experiences for everyone, through a dynamic programme of high quality exhibitions, participatory learning, events and retail.

ABOUT

From small seeds has grown a superb national centre. In the beautiful setting of Navigation Wharf in Sleaford sits an old seed warehouse. But it's not what you'd expect, for this converted warehouse is home to British craft and design.

We are the largest venue in England entirely dedicated to the exhibition, celebration, support and promotion of national and international contemporary craft and design.

Under one roof, our five gallery spaces showcase up to 20 world-class exhibitions every year from the most innovative, challenging and accomplished artists to new and emerging talent.

Our stimulating learning programme inspires people of all ages, skills and interest levels and our shop is a cultural haven for the latest contemporary handmade products.

We are also home to Design Factory and Design Nation supporting British designer-makers in the UK and artsNK, the country's largest rural arts development agency that specialises in visual and performing arts projects.

The National Centre for Craft & Design

The National Centre for Craft & Design
Navigation Wharf, Carre Street, Sleaford
Lincolnshire NG34 7TW

Telephone: +44 (0)1529 308 710

www.nationalcraftanddesign.org.uk